Advancing the TPM Profession

Increase your career path and unlock your potential by successfully leading technical projects.

Epris E. Ezekiel

Copyright 2024© Epris E. Ezekiel
All rights reserved. This book is copyrighted and no part of it may be reproduced, distributed, or transmitted in any form or by any means, including photocopying, recording, or other electronic or mechanical methods, without the prior written permission of the publisher, except in the case of brief quotations embodied in critical reviews and certain other non-commercial uses permitted by copyright law.
Printed in the United States of America Copyright 2024© Epris E. Ezekiel

Contents

History 1
Chapter 1 3
What is TPM, or total productive maintenance? 3
Chapter 2 8
TPM's Four Steps 8
Chapter 3 16
Traditional TPM Foundations 16
Chapter 4 25
OEE and the Six Significant Losses 25
Chapter 5 34
Comprehending the Six Major Setbacks 34
Chapter 6 39
Example of TPM 39
Chapter 7 62
Extra TPM Activities 62
Conclusion 67

History

The TPM system was invented by Japanese inventor Seiichi Nakajima. Upon his "dedication to improving the manufacturing industry," the Emperor bestowed upon him an accolade.

In Japan in the 1950s and 1960s, Nakajima gained expertise with best practices for maintenance, upon which he founded the system. He discovered that efficient operation required a leadership philosophy that included front-line staff in the processes of general improvement.

George Smith, the founder of the Marshall Institute, helped establish the formal procedures and philosophy of total production maintenance (TPM). As a component of Toyota's workflow, TPM significantly reduced equipment-related problems, enabling the evolution of the just-in-time (JIT) strategy for production. Thousands of companies worldwide use TPM today as part of their regimen to maintain operational reliability.

The purpose of overall productive maintenance
Improving the efficiency of machinery and equipment continuously is the sole objective of TPM. Teams that actively contribute to preserving and enhancing efficiency experience TPM.

The effectiveness of Total Productive Maintenance (TPM) as a crucial element of a quality management system can only be fully realized with the cooperation of all teams and individuals involved. It is feasible to achieve TPM's objective with that support in place. The goal of Total Equipment Effectiveness (OEE) improvement for machinery and equipment is the goal of TPM implementation. There are two instant advantages to TPM implementation. It is clearer what is causing the quick decline. Operators might also assume ownership because of the environment.

Chapter 1

What is TPM, or total productive maintenance?

Perfectly functioning machinery, unbroken assembly lines, flawlessly made goods, consistently reached production targets, and timely product pickups and deliveries would all be commonplace. The world isn't ideal, though, regrettably. Events can occur from time to time and cause delays in manufacturing.

TPM, or total productive maintenance, is useful in this situation. To preserve quality and safety across production cycles, TPM advocates for operators to take ownership of the cleaning, upkeep, and improvement of their workstations. To ensure that manufacturing processes run smoothly and without interruptions or delays, TPM aims to maintain equipment in top operating condition.

How does TPM relate to Lean Manufacturing?
TPM, like many other approaches used globally to boost productivity, enhance quality, shorten time to market, and improve workflow, originated in Japan. Since TPM aims to eliminate waste, it is a logical extension of lean manufacturing.

All workers are involved in Total Productive Maintenance, which aims to reduce waste by enhancing manufacturing equipment's functionality, dependability, and efficiency. TPM transfers routine and preventive maintenance accountability from the maintenance team or facilities staff to the equipment operators. This puts the individuals who know the equipment best in charge of ensuring it operates at its best.

The objectives of TPM, when correctly executed, are as follows:
- ✓ A more secure workplace
- ✓ Reduced running expenses

- ✓ Perfect condition
- ✓ Smoother and quicker output
- ✓ No pauses
- ✓ No malfunctions of the equipment

It is like when you do regular maintenance on an automobile. Paying full price to fix a neglected car is more expensive than performing routine maintenance such as rotating the tires, air filter replacement, belt inspections, and oil changes.

Total Productive Maintenance Tools

This sounds terrific, I'm sure, to many of you. How can they put TPM into practice in their firms, though? Exist any procedures that could be beneficial? Thankfully, there are various total productive maintenance technologies available to help facilitate your journey towards Total Productive Maintenance. There will be real tools among them, as well as some software and straightforward but efficient methods. There are numerous approaches to assist a business in completing the goals they have set for itself.

- ❖ **Apply a CMMS.** To help you plan and manage all of your maintenance tasks and procedures, you should consider using a Computerized Maintenance Management System (CMMS) such as MaintainX.
- ❖ **Forms TPM.** All of your information can be organized with the help of standard TPM forms.
- ❖ **Instructional Materials.** Total productive maintenance training is just another example of how training is always a useful tool. Comprehensive training is a good way to gain the buy-in that TPM demands from the entire workforce.
- ❖ **Defining the objectives for overall equipment effectiveness (OEE).** Having a clear, quantifiable goal in mind is important since, as was previously noted, the main aim of TPM is to raise OEE. By monitoring and aggregating your shift-by-shift OEE data for a month, you can establish an objective. To determine your optimal score, multiply your best result by the availability, performance, and

quality components of OEE. The objective that you should strive for is your best score.

❖ **Cards of Inspection.** Brightly colored cards serve as an excellent visual reminder for maintaining current inspection protocols. Vibrantly colored cards can be used to convey how often inspections are conducted. They specify the kind of maintenance required as well as who is accountable.

❖ **Labels.** These cards are another visual tool that operators can use to transmit essential information, similar to the ones discussed above.

Chapter 2

TPM's Four Steps

1. **Increase Knowledge**

    Every organization aspires to function well. They wish to prevent losses brought on by either short-term or long-term equipment breakdowns. When TPM is used, losses become more apparent and people become more conscious.

    Every machine would always be completely operational and generate flawless quality goods if a business operated in a loss-free state where the OEE of all machinery and equipment was 100%. That's where every firm wants to go, to be clear. Nonetheless, it's quite likely that their OEE is less than 50%.

    Recall that achieving a predetermined OEE goal is the aim of TPM. Achieve your objective gradually by setting a reasonable one.

- ✓ How to figure out OEE
- ✓ Quality * Performance * Availability = OEE, where:

- ✓ Run time divided by scheduled production time equals availability.
- ✓ Production Time Allotted – Stop Time Equals Performance
- ✓ Excellent Count / Total Count equals quality.

2. **Never-ending Development**

Usually, overdue maintenance is discovered and completed when tracking the current best outcomes to establish a goal. As such, the entire work floor is cleaned up during this phase of the procedure, which is known as the Total Clean Out. The next stage is to put 5S into practice after this is finished.

The five Japanese terms "5S" (seiri, seiton, seison, seiketsu, shitsuke; translated as "sort," "set in order," "shine," "standardize," and "maintain") stand for particular principles that are used to manage and arrange workplace until it is completely under control and effective. Production of high quality is made possible under this condition. Every workplace should be tidy and orderly, according to S5.

Even though 5s can function on its own, it works far better when combined with other Lean approaches like Kaizen, Lean Six Sigma, and Gemba. Consider the 5s method to be a cycle, in actuality. 5s depends on recurrent duties, which must be recorded for all staff members to adhere to the regular cycle procedure.

Constant Improvement is Provided via CMMS

Managing 5s processes is made easy using a CMMS, which automates operations based on procedures. Process improvement can be streamlined by using a CMMS like MaintainX, which offers a unified platform for digitizing, assigning, and managing standard operating procedures, including your 5s.

It's now time to put the first TPM pillar into practice: continual improvement, after completing Total Clean Out and 5S. By now, a range of disciplines have formed small teams, and they are working to fix any issues that could be affecting their OEE. Small Group Activities, or SGAs, are being carried out by the teams that were constituted. Therefore, in addition to quality inspectors and possibly even logistic managers, the average SGA team will often consist of both mechanics and operators. When the group gets together, they also grow a sense of accountability for the machine or manufacturing line that falls under their jurisdiction.

Ownership

Something of a cultural shift takes place when a team

reaches a point where they feel accountable for the performance of their tools and machinery. Distinctions between "you're the repair technician and I'm the operator" vanish. As a result, a team has been established that understands that, regardless of their specific roles, they all have a responsibility for the equipment's proper operation.

Our shared objective is to maintain optimal operations, and the SGA team will address any problems that emerge in a way that aligns with the Pareto Principle. A theory that goes by the name "80/20 rule" states that 80% of the causes and 20% of the consequences must normally be present. According to TPM, this indicates that only 20% of the computers account for 80% of the losses.

Following their determination of the 20% or the location of the underlying causes, the team will produce a resolution proposal that usually includes a cost-benefit analysis. Whatever the situation, the SGA team can assess if OEE has improved if a remedy is authorized and put into place.

OEE is Gradually Improving

After resolving the original problems, the team proceeds to address any further difficulties that may arise. Furthermore, OEE is gradually improved with each phase. Ultimately, this is simply one step toward TPM, but these actions are repeated in a loop. This is merely the first of eight pillars that make up TPM. Now let us discuss a few of these pillars.

Pillar 2. Maintenance is no longer the exclusive responsibility of experts thanks to the second pillar and the advent of autonomous maintenance. No one is exempt from contributing to maintenance—

technicians, operators, and anybody else with knowledge.

Pillar 3. Creating schedules for predictive as well as preventative maintenance falls under this category.

Pillar 4. More importantly, training is required so that every employee understands the concepts of continuous improvement and Total Productive Maintenance and how they apply to their particular roles.

Pillar 5. The creation of new equipment or processes is addressed by early management. The extent of maintenance procedures that will need to be performed should be considered while selecting new machinery.

Advantages of TBM

Safety. The 5S methodology was discussed previously. There is no doubt that the workplace will be neat, tidy, and safe to work in if and when all five strategies—Sort, Set in Order, Shine, Standardize, and Sustain—have been fully executed.

Even as equipment ages, workplace disruption is becoming less common due to TPM's continuous emphasis on proactive and preventative maintenance. A productive and efficient workplace is frequently safer.

Efficiency. Measuring Overall Equipment Effectiveness (OEE) is critical to putting TPM into play. Efficiency follows from attaining a high OEE since a business aims to have manufacturing lines free from malfunctions, accidents, and mechanical flaws.

Moral. TPM also requires a whole team effort to be successful. All participants must be on board. Additionally, individuals who may have been reluctant to adopt it or even opposed it will probably give up once they realize all of the advantages and improvements. It is now the responsibility of the employees to take care of and maintain their equipment. A sense of pride that the workers may not have previously experienced can result from this.

Satisfaction. Consequently, customer satisfaction has to be the greatest advantage of a comprehensive productive maintenance plan, even though all of the previously listed benefits are significant.

Chapter 3

Traditional TPM Foundations

The five S's serve as the cornerstone of the traditional approach to TPM, which was created in the 1960s and comprises eight supporting activities, also known as pillars.

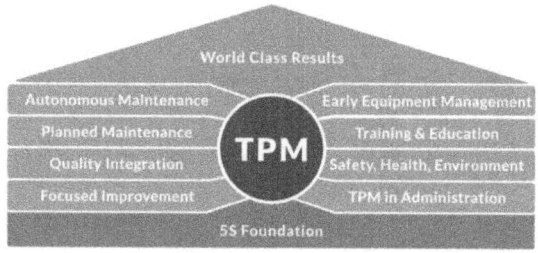

The five S's (Sort, Set in Order, Shine, Standardize, and Sustain) and eight supporting pillars make up the traditional TPM model.

The Foundation for the 5S

Cleaning up, Arranging, Neatness, Discipline, and Ongoing improvement is what Henry T. Ford referred to as the CANDO concept early in the 20th century. About half a century later, Toyota executives came to

Ford to see how they might mass-produce cars.

The CANDO concept impressed the Toyota team, and they modified it to become 5S, or Seiri, Seiton, Seiso, Seiketsu, and Shitsuk. The English translation of these would be "Sort, Set in order, Shine, Standardize, and Sustain"—or the "5 Ss."

Sort

Eliminating unnecessary items from the workspace is the task at hand. For instance, it's critical to get rid of any outdated or damaged equipment that would otherwise obstruct your path. Equipment and materials should also be arranged by frequency of use by operators.

Set in order

Operators in this occupation arrange everything according to its right position. This minimizes wasted time and makes it simple to locate each item rapidly.

Shine

To keep their work area and tools free of dust and grime, operators clean them regularly. Erosion and corrosion brought on by dust and grime accumulation can eventually lead to the breakdown of machinery and other equipment. Because it can assist in preventing accidents and cleaning regularly and safely.

Standardize

Establishing standard operating procedures for carrying out the first three 5S tasks is the task at hand. Every employee must be aware of the requirements and follow them to the letter. Operators can be guaranteed to finish activities by the specified procedures in a standard operating procedures guide by using checklists and audits.

Sustain

Teams should continue to get together regularly even when things are going well to assess and audit the way things are currently being done and identify areas for improvement.

The basis that 5S builds for well-functioning equipment should be quite obvious. Tools and parts, for instance, are much easier to locate in a neat and orderly workspace, and new problems like fluid leaks, material spills, metal shavings from unanticipated wear, tiny cracks in gears, etc. are also very visible.

The 8 Pillars of TPM

Proactive and preventive methods for enhancing equipment reliability are the main focus of the eight TPM pillars.

Autonomous Maintenance

The machines and equipment that operators use daily need to be regularly cleaned, lubricated, inspected and maintained. This frees up maintenance staff to work on more urgent tasks, encourages employees to take responsibility for the equipment they use, and teaches them more about how it works.

What Benefits Does It Offer?

- ✓ Allows maintenance staff to focus on more complex jobs.
- ✓ Detects emerging problems before they turn into catastrophes.
- ✓ Make ensuring the equipment is properly oiled and cleaned.
- ✓ Improves the understanding of operators on their machinery.
- ✓ Increases the "ownership" that operators have over their machinery.

Planned Maintenance

On schedules determined by projected or previously recorded equipment failure rates, planned or preventative maintenance is carried out. Age and usage statistics of the machine are also factored into planned maintenance. Preventing unscheduled downtime and machine failure is the goal of this kind of maintenance.

What Benefits Does It Offer?

- ✓ Controls wear-and failure-prone parts more effectively, thereby reducing inventory.

- Lowers the number of unscheduled stop times significantly.
- Allows most maintenance to be scheduled for periods when the machinery isn't expected to be used.

Quality maintenance

This entails keeping an eye on machine performance to identify and stop equipment malfunctions while they're in use. Employees can work on other projects by using automated programs to complete them. Perform a root cause analysis to find and fix the issue when errors occur.

What Benefits Does It Offer?

- Lowers costs by the early detection of flaws (defects cannot always be reliably and expensively found through inspection).
- Focuses improvement programs on eliminating the underlying causes of faults to specifically target quality issues.
- Minimizes the number of flaws.

Focused improvement

To find and eliminate anything that does not improve the production process or the end product, small groups of stakeholders examine the activities involved in the process. The goal of this approach is to keep making equipment operations better.

What Benefits Does It Offer?
- ✓ Bring a company's capabilities together to form a machine that is always improving.
- ✓ Cross-functional teams are tasked with identifying and fixing recurring issues.

Early equipment management

Equipment is designed with advancements made possible by experience and information gained from prior production and maintenance operations. Make sure that new machinery can achieve expected performance levels by collaborating with other stakeholders, suppliers, and equipment makers.

What Benefits Does It Offer?
- ✓ The practical review and employee involvement before installation make maintenance easier and more reliable.

- ✓ Because there are fewer startup problems with new equipment, anticipated performance levels are reached considerably faster.

Training and Education

For the firm to achieve its objectives, all staff members—from operators to senior management—need to receive training in TPM approaches. This will ensure that there are no knowledge gaps.

What Benefits Does It Offer?

- ✓ In addition to employee coaching and development, TPM principles are taught to managers.
- ✓ Operators learn how to spot new issues and perform routine maintenance on the machinery.
- ✓ Prevention and proactive maintenance methods are taught to maintenance staff.

Environment, health, and safety

One essential component of TPM is creating a workplace that is safe and healthy for every employee. Workers who feel safe and well-groomed exhibit better moods and are more productive. Maintaining a secure workplace reduces the number of accidents that occur there

What Benefits Does It Offer?
- ✓ Focuses in particular on the objective of having no workplace accidents.
- ✓ Reduces the possibility of hazards to health and safety, making the workplace safer.

TPM in administration

Beyond the manufacturing floor, TPM principles ought to be used. Managers, administrators, and employees can use TPM approaches in the workplace to cut waste and boost productivity. People can use TPM, for instance, to assess if all of the scheduled meetings are necessary.

What Benefits Does It Offer?
- ✓ Enhances administrative functions to support production (e.g., order processing, procurement, and scheduling).
- ✓ TPM extends its benefits beyond the factory floor by tackling waste in administrative processes.

Chapter 4

OEE and the Six Significant Losses

Outline of OEE

The OEE (Overall Equipment Effectiveness) statistic indicates true productivity in scheduled production time. Through precise tracking of the path toward "perfect production," it was designed to assist TPM programs.

- ✓ Manufacturers without TPM or lean initiatives frequently have an OEE score of 40%.
- ✓ For discrete producers, an OEE score of 60% is reasonably average.
- ✓ For discrete manufacturers, an OEE score of 85% represents the best in the world.
- ✓ Perfect production is indicated by an OEE score of 100%.

The three fundamental components of OEE account for three distinct types of productivity loss and correspond to one of the TPM goals outlined at the beginning of this issue.

Component	TPM Goal	Kind of Loss in Productivity
Availability	No Stops	All events that halt planned production for a significant amount of time (usually several minutes or more) are included in Availability Loss, which is factored into the calculation of availability. The two types of stops are scheduled (like changeovers) and unplanned (like

		breakdowns and other downtime incidents).
Performance	Avoiding brief pauses and running slowly	Performance covers all the elements that lead to production running at a speed lower than its maximum potential. Performance Loss is the result of these factors. The two types of examples are small stops and slow cycles.

Quality	No Defects	Rework and other manufactured components that don't meet quality standards are taken into account by Quality Loss, which is a component of quality. Two instances are lower yield at startup and production rejects.
OEE	Perfect	To calculate a

	Production	measure of genuinely productive manufacturing time, OEE accounts for all three types of losses: availability, performance, and quality.

No Breakdowns (measured by Availability), No Small Stops or Slow Running (measured by Performance), and No Defects (measured by Quality) are the TPM goals that are closely linked to OEE, as the above table shows.

To identify and assess productivity losses as well as to monitor and measure the gains brought about by TPM programs, it is critical to measure OEE.

Benefits of OEE Tracking Automatically

Doing an OEE calculation by hand is a fantastic place to start. Five pieces of data (planned production time, stop time, ideal cycle time, total count, and good count) are required, and they can be completed using pen and paper or a basic spreadsheet. Manually calculating OEE offers a greater knowledge of the idea and serves to reinforce it. But switching to automated OEE data collecting as soon as possible also has some very significant advantages:

Item	Benefit
Stop Time	According to experience from numerous firms, the accuracy of manually measuring unscheduled halt times is usually between 60 and 80%. Run/Down automatic detection can increase this accuracy to about 100%.

Small Stops and Slow Cycles	Handling slow cycles and short stops is not feasible for most equipment. Consequently, a significant amount of potentially valuable data, including loss patterns based on time and events, is not accessible.
Focus on Operators	Handling slow cycles and short stops is not feasible for most equipment. Consequently, a significant amount of potentially valuable data, including loss patterns based on time and events, is not accessible.

Results in Real-Time	Improved methods like SIC (Short Interval Control) are made possible by automated data collecting, which yields results instantly.

Establishing a "Best of the Best" OEE Objective

How to establish a "stretch" goal for OEE that works is an intriguing subject. Fortunately, there is a very good method for achieving the "Best of the Best." This is how it functions:

1. Monitor OEE for the target equipment for a month, taking into account Performance, Availability, and Quality. Achieve proper results compilation by shift.

2. Examine the results of each shift, noting the best individual outcomes for Performance, Quality, and Availability (that is, the highest Performance score, the highest Availability score, etc.) across the course of all shifts.

3. To acquire a "Best of the Best" OEE score, multiply all of the top individual performances together.

The stretch goal, which is based on the best real results for Availability, Performance, and Quality during the month, is represented by this newly computed "Best of the Best" OEE score.

Chapter 5

Comprehending the Six Major Setbacks

The most frequent reasons for lost productivity in manufacturing are known as the Six Big Losses, and they can be further subdivided into the OEE loss categories of availability loss, performance loss, and quality loss. The significance of The Six Big Losses lies in their almost universal applicability to discrete production and their excellent foundation for considering, recognizing, and combating waste (i.e., productivity loss).

Six Big Losses	Category OEE	Examples	Comments
Unexpected Breaks	Availability Decrease	Unplanned Maintenance, Warm Bearing, Motor Failure,	The line between an Unplanned Stop

		and Tool Failure	(Availability Loss) from a Small Stop (Performance Loss) might be drawn anywhere.
Configuration and Modifications	Loss of Availability	Warm-up Time, Setup/Changeover, Material Shortage, Operator Shortage, Significant Adjustment	Programs like SMED, which reduce setup time, are frequently used to mitigate

			this loss (Single-Minute Exchange of Die).
Small Stops	Diminished Performance	Sensor Blocked, Delivery Blocked, Minor Adjustment, Component Jam, Cleaning/Checking	Generally, only stops lasting under five minutes and do not require maintenance staff to be included.
Slow	Diminish	Misalignment,	Somethin

Running	ed Performance	Gear Wear, and Inaccurate Configuration	g that prevents the machinery from operating at its optimum theoretical speed.
Production Errors	Poor Quality Loss	Trash, Redesign	Rejects in the production process at a steady state.
Lower	Poor	Trash,	Rejects

Yield	Quality Loss	Redesign	from early production, warm-up, or starting.

Chapter 6

Example of TPM

Going through an implementation example is a great method to gain a greater knowledge of TPM. An easy-to-follow implementation roadmap for TPM is provided in this section.

Step 1: Determine the Pilot Area

The target equipment for the TPM program pilot is chosen in this step. There are three reasonable methods to go about making this choice.

Which Tools?	Benefits	Negative
Most Simple to Enhance	. Kinder to those with less TPM experience. . Ideal	. Less rigorously than the other alternatives "tests" the TPM

	circumstance for a "short win".	process.
		. Not as beneficial as upgrading the equipment used for limitation.
Bottleneck or Restraint	. The quickest payback is offered. . Boosts overall productivity right away.	. Equipment that is enhanced can end up being offline more often than anticipated. . A higher-risk option is to

		work on a key asset as a pilot project.
The most problematic	. Operator support will be strong for equipment improvement. . Resolving well-known issues will increase support for the TPM initiative.	. Unsolved problems frequently remain unsolved for a purpose: obtaining satisfactory results may be difficult. . Less return than enhancing equipment for

		constraints.

Here are a few more rules to follow:

- ✓ Teams frequently prefer to pick the Most Problematic equipment. But unless it's also the Constraint/Bottleneck, this is rarely the best option.
- ✓ The Constraint/Bottleneck equipment is nearly always the best option for a business with moderate to strong TPM knowledge and/or support (from internal workers or outside consultants). The goal is to limit potential risk by developing temporary stock and generally ensuring that unforeseen stop time may be endured.
- ✓ Typically, the easiest equipment to improve is the greatest option for a business with little TPM help (from external consultants or internal workers).

Ensure that all relevant employees—operators, maintenance staff, and managers—are included in the selection process to get broad support for the TPM project. Additionally, endeavor to reach a consensus within the group regarding the equipment selection.

After the pilot area has been chosen, establish a local visual focal point for the project (such as a project board) where updates on plans and progress can be shared.

Step 2: Get the Equipment Back in Top Working Order

The equipment will be cleaned and generally prepared for better performance in this step. We'll start with two essential TPM ideas:

- ✓ 5S
- ✓ Self-Sustained Upkeep

The first step should be to start a 5S program that involves operators and maintenance staff.

Item	Description
Photograph	Post the photos you take of the equipment on the project board to show it in its original condition.
Vacant Space	Make sure everything is clear of any unnecessary objects, debris, and extra tools and parts.
Prepare	Arrange the last of

		the tools and materials on shadow boards, which are boards with outlines used as visual indicators.
	Clean Up	Ensure everything is clean, including any spills or leaks, the surrounding area, and the equipment.
	Photograph	Pictures demonstrating the equipment's improved condition are uploaded to the project board.

List of Things	Make a basic 5S checklist for the region (establishing Standardized Work inside the 5S process).
Audit	Plan a routine audit to ensure that the 5S checklist is being followed. Start the audit daily, then every week. To maintain the checklist up to date and applicable, make necessary updates throughout the audit. Maintain

	an upbeat and inspiring atmosphere during audits (consider them a kind of training).

It is then necessary to start an autonomous maintenance program. Aim to establish a consensus amongst operators and maintenance staff over what routine chores can be completed effectively by operators. Raising the competence level of operators will often necessitate some minor training.

Item	Description
Checkpoints for Inspection	List all wear parts together with the important inspection sites and record them. If you want visual help, think about

	making a map of inspection points.
Observance	If there is any opaque guarding that obstructs inspection points, replace it with transparent guarding (if practical and safe).
Points Set	Every set point should be identified and its settings should be recorded. As a visual help for inspection and auditing, think about marking settings directly on the apparatus.

Lubrication Points	List every lubrication point that you can find. To prevent unplanned stop times, schedule lubrication to happen during changeovers or other scheduled stops. If it is practical and safe to do so, think about externalizing lubrication sites that are hard to reach or that involve halting the machinery.
Instruction for Operators	Employees should be instructed to notify the line supervisor of any anomalies or newly discovered circumstances.

Establish a Checklist	For all operator-controlled maintenance operations, such as lubrication, set points, and inspections, create a basic Autonomous Maintenance checklist (establishing Standardized Work for the Autonomous Maintenance process).
Audit	Plan an audit to confirm that the Autonomous Maintenance checklist is being followed regularly (weekly at first, then daily). Keep the checklist up to date and pertinent by making necessary updates throughout the

	audit. Treat audits like a training activity by keeping them upbeat and inspiring.

Step 3: Begin Assessing OEE

A system is implemented in this step to monitor OEE for the equipment that is the goal. The scope of the system must include unscheduled halt time reason code tracking. The system can be automated (such as Vorne's XL Productivity ApplianceTM) or manual (see www.oee.com for complete instructions on completing manual OEE calculations).

Unplanned stop times cause the majority of equipment's losses to be greatest. So that you can see where productive time is being lost, it is highly advised that you classify each unexpected halt event. Furthermore, a category for "unallocated" stop times—

that is, halt times for which the cause is uncertain—should be included. For manually recorded OEE, it is particularly crucial to include a category for unallocated halt time. Because it gives operators a safe choice in cases where the rationale for the stop time is unclear, it increases accuracy.

Two weeks or more of data collection are required to determine the impact of minor stops and slow cycles, as well as to discover recurrent causes for equipment unscheduled halt times. Make sure the data is correct and that the real reasons for unscheduled stop times are being recorded by going over it with the supervisor throughout each shift.

Step 4: Deal with Significant Losses

The biggest causes of wasted productive time are dealt with in this stage. Introduced is the TPM idea of Focused Improvement, or Kaizen.

Item	Description

Choose Loss	Choose one significant loss to rectify based on data on stop times and OEE unique to the equipment. Generally speaking, the largest source of unscheduled stop time should be the major loss that is chosen.
Build a Team	To tackle the issue, form a cross-functional team. The four to six workers on this team should include supervisors, maintenance staff, and operators with the most equipment knowledge and expertise and they should get along well with one another.
Get Data	Gather comprehensive data about the problem's symptoms,

	including observations, tangible proof, and pictures. When gathering data, think about utilizing an Ishikawa (fishbone) diagram at the apparatus.
Put Together	Plan a systematic approach to issue solving with the following objectives: a) determine the problem's likely causes; b) assess the likely causes in light of the information acquired; and c) choose the best solutions.
Plan	Set a scheduled stop time to apply the suggested corrections. Make careful to use the current change control procedure if one exists when applying patches.

Restart	After a suitable amount of time, resume production and assess the fixes' efficacy. After a treatment has been modified and proven to be effective enough, proceed to the next significant loss. If not, gather more data and schedule another structured problem-solving meeting.

To track the progress of losses that have previously been rectified and to keep an eye on overall productivity gains, OEE data should be meticulously examined during each shift during this phase.

Step 5: Explain Preventive Maintenance Methods

The TPM idea of planned maintenance is introduced in this stage by incorporating proactive maintenance procedures into the maintenance schedule.

To begin with, list every part that should be maintained proactively:

Item	Description
Parts That Get Worn	All wearable parts should be identified and recorded; these should have been set up as inspection locations in Step Two. Examine substituting worn components with ones that have little or no wear.
Parts That Break	Compile a list of all the parts that are known to malfunction frequently

Stress Areas	To get more information about the stress spots in your equipment, think about using vibration analysis and/or thermography.

Next, set up the first intervals for preventive maintenance:

Item	Description
Dependent on Wear	Determine the baseline replacement interval and the present wear level of wear components (in some situations, an early replacement may be prompted by an Autonomous Maintenance inspection,

	as defined in Step Two).
Based on Expected Failure	Establish a baseline (anticipated) failure interval for components that are prone to failure.
Temporary-Based	Establish a baseline. a planned maintenance schedule that calls for the proactive replacement of any part that is prone to wear and failure. As an alternative to "Calendar Time," think about utilizing "Run Time" as the interval time base.

Work Order-Based	Establish a uniform procedure for creating work orders using the planned maintenance schedule as a guide.

Next, develop a feedback mechanism to maximize the intervals between maintenance:

Item	Description
Log of Components	For every component that is prone to wear and failure, create a Component Log sheet. Keep track of each replacement incident and the component's status (e.g., wear amount, "component failed," "no observable issues," etc.) at

	the time of replacement.
Every Month's Audit	Conduct a monthly audit of planned maintenance, making sure to: a) confirm that the schedule is being followed; b) confirm that the component log sheets are being kept up to date; and c) examine all new entries in the component log and, if necessary, modify the maintenance intervals. Treat audits like a training activity by keeping them upbeat and inspiring.
Modifications to	Whenever an unforeseen

Maintenance Intervals	component replacement occurs, think about modifying the maintenance interval. Think about including the component if it isn't already on the planned maintenance schedule.
Analysis of Components	To identify new concerns and problems, think about charting data from vibration analysis and thermography over time.

Chapter 7

Extra TPM Activities

The Simplified Roadmap is designed to offer a gradual, methodical approach to TPM implementation. So, what comes next in the TPM journey?

There are four more TPM tasks that are outside the purview of the Simplified roadmap. So, when should these activities be introduced? Becomes the question. Prioritizing the selection of new activities should be done by the incremental, step-by-step method, taking into account the most immediate and pressing demand.

TPM Activity	Introduce When...
Quality Maintenance	Top of the list among the company's concerns is quality. There could be two possible reasons for this: either a) major consumer complaints about quality, or b)

	major internal complaints about quality (such as an inadequate first-pass yield).
Early Equipment Administration	In a restricted or bottleneck location, new equipment is being built or installed.
Environment, Health, and Safety	The organization either a) lacks a major Safety, Health, and Environment program, or b) the program that is in place would greatly benefit from integration with current TPM initiatives.

TPM in Executive Roles One of the biggest obstacles to manufacturing running well is administrative issues (e.g., delays in processing customer orders or bills, and problems with part procurement).

Durable Enhancement

How to produce lasting progress is one of the biggest problems each firm faces. This covers both a) attaining immediate success and b) sustaining that success in the long run. Four methods for accomplishing long-term progress are described in this section.

- ✓ To prevent the program from being stale or the staff from growing complacent, evolving the project uses continuous improvement strategies. Remaining innovative and engaging is the aim of the endeavor. The project's ongoing adaptation to a changing environment is another way that evolving it helps guarantee its long-term success.

- ✓ Senior management, especially the Plant Manager, has the primary duty of exercising active leadership. It entails consistently showcasing, in both words and deeds, the significance of TPM operations. Employees' inclination to revert to their previous work habits and behavioral patterns is fought by proactive leadership. Employees eventually adopt these new, deeply ingrained behaviors as a result of the initiative's constant infusion of fresh energy.

- ✓ Initiatives must involve employees if they are to succeed in the near and long term. Developing a shared picture of the "improved" state of the business and stating how it would benefit staff members is a potent strategy for motivating workers. A powerful, all-encompassing drive to succeed will result from this. Identifying and rewarding desirable behavior is another effective tactic. Giving out a monthly trophy for the best 5S area or monthly gift cards for the largest kaizen improvement are two examples of this in the context of TPM.

- ✓ Early success gives the project more momentum, which increases the likelihood of long-term success. On the other hand, it will be considerably more difficult to carry out an initiative in the future if it is thought to have been tried and unsuccessful.

Conclusion

Completely productive maintenance is a comprehensive maintenance strategy that maximizes performance, lowers the chance of failure, and increases production. A TPM program, which is founded on the ideas of autonomous and preventative maintenance, necessitates the active participation of all employees and managers. TPM promotes effective team communication and a culture of continuous development.

In summary, this is the location where the maintenance of equipment and the manufacturing process are integrated. Though in practice it may not seem like a difficult process, it is. Plus, the advantages much exceed any early drawbacks.

www.ingramcontent.com/pod-product-compliance
Lightning Source LLC
Chambersburg PA
CBHW070409230526
45471CB00006B/2718